An aerial view of the Normandy Landings

Text and photography Orville Castaire
Translation Ben Warren

Cover.
Pointe du Hoc, at low tide, topped with a monument in memory of the men of the 116th US infantry regiment.

Illustrations.
Pegasus Bridge.
American Military Cemetery, Colleville-sur-Mer.
Concrete caissons towed from England to construct the dykes.

4th on cover.
Sainte-Mère-Eglise, the church tower and the parachutist.

Editions OUEST-FRANCE

Overlord, birth of an armada

On the continent, the Nazis' victory appeared total. To the West only Britain remained defiantly non-German. To the East, with the German-Soviet pact broken, Stalin, who had been forced to retreat to the Don, called for help and asked for a new Western Front to be created to reduce pressure on the USSR. However, by the beginning of 1943, the tide of battle was slowly turning.

The entry of the United States into the war in 1941 began to shift the balance of power. In Europe, the British were working at building up their air force and the increased range of its bombers made it possible to attack the large German cities. The RAF planned to destroy all of the Nazi munitions factories. The Americans continued their strikes too, so that Germany started to have a shortage of equipment. Consequently, the Luftwaffe was barely able to secure its own skies, let alone those of the countries it had occupied. The fightback also continued at sea, as Churchill and Roosevelt decided to take back control of the Pacific, the Mediterranean and the Atlantic. By the second half of 1943 they had succeeded. Germany had lost the maritime advantage. Even if the Third Reich remained the dominating power, its retreat had begun.

From spring 1942, in order to reduce German pressure on the Russians and thereby avoid any new German-Soviet agreement, an Anglo-Soviet treaty was signed, followed shortly afterward by an American-Soviet agreement, based on the principle of opening a second Allied Front in Europe.

The Russians, spurred into action, engaged in some extremely violent battles that saw the surrender of General Paulus near Stalingrad in February 1943 and a redrawing of the battle lines further East. The Soviets took back the initiative and gave the Germans a rough ride, forcing them to commit two-thirds of their forces to the Eastern flanks.

At the Casablanca Conference in January 1943, Churchill and Roosevelt agreed on the principle of the landings. This large-scale operation was to take place on the Northwest coast of France, it was

Casablanca Conference, January 24 1943. (Taken from *Les plages du débarquement*, Yves Lecouturier, Éd. Ouest-France)

The Allied heads of state: seated, from left to right: Tedder, Eisenhower, Montgomery. Standing, from left to right: Bradley, Ramsay, Leigh-Mallory, Bedell-Smith. (I.W.M. document) (Taken from *6 juin 1944, débarquement en Normandie*, Général Compagnon, Éd. Ouest-France)

decided in Washington in May and the scheme was finalised in Quebec the following August. In Cairo in December 1943, Roosevelt suggested that the operation should be led by General Eisenhower.

The last days of 1943 saw the Allied leaders, Churchill, Roosevelt and Stalin meet, for the first time, in Tehran. Stalin's troops had just won some significant victories on the Eastern Front and this put the Russian leader in a strong negotiating position. He managed to veto the British plans for a Central European offensive starting in Italy (not wanting any forays into his sphere of influence) and got confirmation that the landings would take place in France in 1944. (For good measure he also persuaded the Allied leaders to allow him to divide up Poland after victory had been assured.)

The invasion would, therefore, take place in Normandy, more specifically on the Calvados coast, which could be accessed from Britain. By bombing the bridges that spanned the Seine and the Loire, the region could be isolated, preventing any possible German reinforcements from arriving. Moreover, most importantly, it was a favourable location because Hitler was convinced that the invasion would take place on the Pas-de-Calais coast.

In December 1943 Eisenhower, who had been named chief of the Expeditionary Forces, took charge of the operation. The assault on Europe was to be launched with the biggest armada the world had ever seen. The operation would involve assembling some 3 million men, the construction of transport boats and landing craft in large numbers and the building of temporary artificial harbours that would have to be towed across the English Channel. All the time, while trying to disguise this massive operation from the Germans, the Americans and British mobilised, trained and prepared their men. Meanwhile, on the French coast, the Germans were not resting on their laurels. The Atlantic Wall was being reinforced with blockhouses, munitions, radars, underwater obstacles and, on the beaches, mines…

The Atlantic Wall

The Germans, who had succeeded in cracking the Allied codes, knew that an Anglo-American landing was being prepared. What they did not know, however, was where and when…

Convinced of their superiority on land, the Germans were split between two strategies on how best to protect the coastline. Marshall Von Rundstedt believed in the mobility of his troops, in particular the infamous *Panzerdivisions*. He considered the blockhouses of the Atlantic Wall to be of little use in stopping an Allied landing. "A mere bluff," he said. "Let the enemy land and then we can attack them with armoured tanks: this will cause them greater losses." This plan, he hoped, would avoid him having to disperse most of his troops along the entire length of the coast. Moreover, he was convinced that an operation could only take place on the Pas-de-Calais coastline, where there were numerous deep-water ports that were easily accessible from Britain.

Field-Marshall Rommel, who had been given responsibility for the overall defence of the French coast, had a somewhat different perspective and considered the Normandy coast to be the most exposed. "The first 24 hours are decisive. It is therefore necessary to prevent any initial landing," he said. When he took command, he discovered the inactivity of Von Rundstedt in completing the "Atlantic Wall" and instantly set about significantly reinforcing the coastal defences. He increased the number and strength of the fortifications and, in particular, transformed the beaches into a series of deadly traps for any would-be attackers. Rommel increased the firepower concentrated at the beaches, created tank traps to destroy any potential landing craft, built concrete barriers and dug trenches and anti-tank ditches as well as laying some 5 million mines. By June 1944, the workers under the command of chief engineer Fritz, who was responsible for the construction on the Wall, had already completed two thirds of the planned defences. However, the Western Front, considered by Berlin to barely active, was scaled back in favour of other combat zones, in particular to help repel the Allied landings in Italy, on 22 January 1944.

German propaganda leaflet from 1943. (Propaganda Staffel) (Taken from *6 juin 1944, débarquement en Normandie*, Général Compagnon, Éd. Ouest-France)

Beaches littered with obstacles placed by the Germans including ramps, mined stakes and tetrahedrons, and all lined with mines. (E.C.P.A. document) (Taken from *6 juin 1944, débarquement en Normandie*, Général Compagnon, Éd. Ouest-France)

Blockhouses, bunkers and pillboxes of the Atlantic Wall stretching along the length of the Normandy coast. On the left, at Colleville-sur-Mer, the support centre W.N. 62. Right, looking East to Pointe du Hoc.

Bottom:
Blockhouses concealed in the vegetation and the launch ramp for the V-1 (this one, at Eperlecques in the Pas-de-Calais).

On the Normandy front line, Rommel had at his command some 40,000 men and 500 armoured tanks. Over the 200 kilometres that separate Antifer from Barfleur, there were more than a thousand fortifications of various types (command posts, blockhouses, gun emplacements, radar stations) and 150 powerful cannons. The most formidable gun batteries were located, from West to East, at La Pernelle, the Saint-Marcouf islands, Pointe du Hoc, Longues-sur-Mer, Merville and Le Havre.

Firestorm

By the time D-Day arrived, there were nearly 3 million men actively involved in the war for the Allies; Americans, Britons, Canadians, Poles, French, Belgians, Norwegians, Czechs, Dutch and over a million men from the Commonwealth countries. That night, the weather conditions were so bad that the Germans believed that the Allies will not dare to attempt anything so Field-Marshall Rommel took the opportunity to return to Berlin to celebrate his wife's birthday.

June 5 1944 and night had barely fallen when hundreds of small aeroplanes took off, some towing gliders. Some 23,000 British and American advance scouts were parachuted behind the German lines to prepare the ground, in particular, their mission was to silence the gun batteries and DCA (the infamous FLAK positions), as well as to mark out the landing zones for the gliders.

On June 6, at 12.20am, 180 men in six gliders from the British 6th airborne division landed on a stone jetty besides the bridge spanning the channel between Caen and the sea. They knew the territory and their mission by heart as they had been practicing over a period of two months on a full-scale model. The bridge, which became famous as the Pegasus Bridge, was captured within six minutes. Then it was the turn of the bridge over the Orne, linking Ranville with Bénouville. From that point on, the Germans were cut off from reinforcements coming from the East or South. Two hours later, Ranville became the first liberated French village.

Almost simultaneously, some 15,000 parachutists from the American 101st and 82nd airborne divisions were released just East of the Douve river, near the village of Sainte-Mère-Eglise. Their mission was to clear the ground up to the coast and the beaches, which, from then on, was codenamed Utah Beach. The landing was difficult, coming down in woodland and marshy pasture that had been flooded by Field-Marshall Rommel. Losses were considerable, in terms of men and equipment. Only 6,000 men survive to face the Germans. Just before daybreak, another 50 gliders landed to the Northwest of Saint-Mère-Eglise, liberated the small town and assumed control of the bridges over the Merderet and the Douve rivers.

From midnight, more than 1,000 British bombers began to unleash 6,000 tonnes of bombs on the coastal positions between the Orne and the Douve. This deluge of fire and iron lasted until 6.30am, when the first men set foot on the Normandy coast. The aerial bombardment was responsible for the destruction of more than three quarters of the German radar stations. On their side, the French Resistance also stepped into action, sabotaging the main telephone lines, bridges and road signs. Yet despite these signs, for several more hours, German High command had its doubts. This was not, it believed, the large-scale landing they had been waiting for.

Pegasus Bridge, linking the Caen channel to the sea. A replica has since been built.

A whole night of bombing and a day of attacks created deep ravines in the ground and eroded the cliff.

Left: **L.S.T. ("Landing Ship Tan") laden,** ready to disembark. Note the anti-aircraft barrage balloons intended as obstacles for enemy aeroplanes. (R.H.A. document) (Taken from *6 juin 1944, débarquement en Normandie*, Général Compagnon, Éd. Ouest-France)

Right: **American troops aboard an L.C.I. heading for Utah on 6 June 1944,** under the protection of barrage balloons intended to thwart the approach of enemy aeroplanes. (R.H.A. document) (Taken from *6 juin 1944, débarquement en Normandie*, Général Compagnon, Éd. Ouest-France)

The longest day

From the end of May, all of the forces involved in Operation Overlord were gathered near the ports of the Southeast coast of Britain and, by June 1, the men were ready to go to war. Arms, vehicles and men began to be loaded on to the ships ready for the crossings. It seemed all the more unreal for taking place during a real storm. A depression over Ireland was slowly moving South, however, a slight calm was expected on June 6.

June 4 and vessels converge towards the South of the Isle of Wight.

June 5. The biggest armada of all time was united at a site nicknamed "Piccadilly Circus" and set off towards the French coast. In front, minesweepers cleared the route. Six battleships, two monitors, twenty-two cruisers and ninety-three destroyers provided support. Finally, at the rear, 7,000 boats of all types moved forward through treacherous seas. On board were more than 300,000 men.

During the night of June 5, and into the morning of the next day, thousands of planes set off to attack the German positions. Seventy-four of the 92 enemy radar stations were destroyed. Simultaneously, the warships worked together to bombard the Atlantic Wall with thousands of shells.

At 3am, the first vessels arrived in the holding zone, some ten miles from the coast. Heavily laden, the men took their places on board the landing crafts that, at a speed of four or five knots, brave the difficult weather conditions.

In front of them, France was known only by the codenames of the five beaches where they were due to set foot: Utah, named after the men of the American 7th army corps, Omaha for the American 5th army corps, Gold for the British 50th infantry division, Juno for the Canadian 3rd infantry division and Sword for the British 3rd division. Amongst the ranks of the latter, 117 French marine fusiliers, the Kieffer commando, the only representatives of the Free French in the operation.

Utah Beach

Utah Beach was the only landing point situated in the French department of Manche. In the Allies' strategy, it played a key role: no matter what happens elsewhere, this place had to be captured at all costs. In the event of general failure on the other landing sites, it would be the starting point for "Plan B", which would reattempt the invasion from the freed Cotentin peninsula.

The area was defended by the powerful Saint-Marcouf battery, one of the strongest defences that the Allies had to encounter. With 25-kilometre-range cannons, it covered the area from Saint-Vaast-la-Hougue to the bay of Veys, at the mouth of the Douve. Despite being violently bombarded from the air and the sea, during the night of June 5-6, it wouldn't be abandoned by the Germans until June 12.

At 6.30am, having been tossed around by mountainous seas, General Collins' men reached the coast, but some 2 kilometres from the intended spot. The Varreville dunes were their intended destination but it was at La Madeleine, a less defended zone, that the first wave lands, led by Brigadier-General Theodore Roosevelt, cousin of the American President. As a result there were limited losses in terms of men as well as equipment. And so the 33-tonne Sherman tanks were soon made operational.

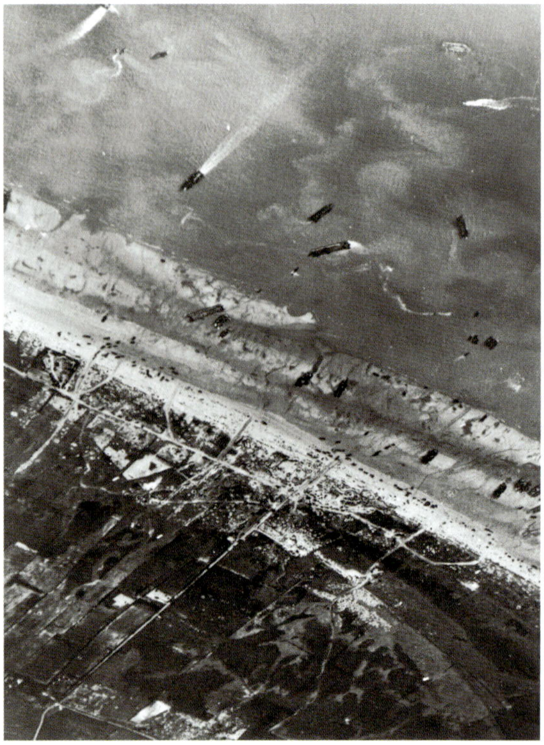

D-Day at Utah Beach. (Taken from *6 juin 1944, débarquement en Normandie*, Général Compagnon, Éd. Ouest-France)

Bottom left:
La Madeleine, Landings museum and monument to the US 4th division (7th corps).

Below: **La Madeleine,** a monument to the 1st Engineer Special brigade and a stele in memory of the 90th infantry division, at Sainte-Marie-du-Mont.

At 8am, the main offensive began. Some 30,000 men and 3,500 vehicles had been landed and the dunes were soon crossed. By midday, the four "beach exits" were in the hands of the liberators. Soon after, at Pouppeville, the German command post that supported the fortified points of the zone, the troops met up with the parachutists who had been dropped off during the night inland and who had recaptured Sainte-Mère-Eglise.

Top: **The dunes at Varreville.**

Bottom: **Varreville,** monument to General Leclerc and the 2nd Armoured Division.

Top: **H-Hour at Omaha Beach,** Easy Green sector, 116th infantry regiment of the 29th US infantry division. (R.H.A. document) (Taken from *6 juin 1944, débarquement en Normandie*, Général Compagnon, Éd. Ouest-France)

Bloody Omaha Beach

The objective assigned to the American 1st infantry division was to establish itself behind the coast along a line leading from Isigny-sur-Mer to Vaucelles (the entrance to Bayeux). In order to do this, General Omar Bradley's men had to spread themselves along the 6.5 kilometres of narrow beaches bounded both East and West by 30-metre-high limestone cliffs, between the point of la Percée and the beach of Colleville-sur-Mer. The Germans had built numerous lookout posts there, including, to the North, (and 6 kilometres from Omaha Beach), the famous battery of Pointe du Hoc. But it proved to not pose a problem for the Americans: painstakingly bombarded, it was neutralised by daybreak on June 6, by 255 men from Colonel Rudder's US Rangers battalion. The batteries of Vierville-sur-Mer, Saint-Laurent and Colleville-sur-Mer, on the other hand, would cause severe damage with their machine-gunners, mortars, flame-throwers and anti-tank guns.

At 4.30am, the landing craft were launched some 10 kilometres from the coast. The sea was very rough. The barges, previously considered unsinkable, do sink under their load. The men were saved but 27 amphibious Sherman tanks were lost.

At 6.30am, when the GIs attempted to set foot

29th infantry division in front of Colleville-sur-Mer, June 6 1944. (Taken from *Les plages du débarquement*, Yves Lecouturier, Éd. Ouest-France)

Vierville-sur-Mer and Colleville-sur-Mer, below, were defended by impressive batteries.

on land, they found themselves under a deluge of fire coming from the 85 blockhouses that had survived the bombardments. They had to cross hell before finding, 200 metres further on, the illusion of shelter behind the rubble that enclosed the beach. This rubble, consisting mainly of large pebbles, became an uncrossable barrier for the heavy equipment, without bulldozers to clear a passage. The 1st infantry division, made famous by its nickname "The Big Red One" since proving its courage in Sicily and North Africa, folds. By 7.30am, some 2,500 men had died.

At 9am, after fierce combat, the Germans finally conceded some ground. The first support post was captured, but not enough headway had been made. In despair, General Bradley orders the navy to start firing, despite the danger to his men. The firepower of the Germans was weakened.

At midday, the units regrouped and advanced. Vierville-sur-Mer was captured, followed by Colleville-sur-Mer.

By the time night fell, the two camps were exhausted. Battle had ceased. There had been more than 3,000 American deaths and just as many injured. But the Germans were beginning to run low of ammunition and, throughout the night, flairs and rockets were fired by the Allied air force to prevent them from sending reinforcements to the area now know as Bloody Omaha Beach.

Pointe du Hoc

Pointe du Hoc is a beauty spot and is worth a detour for its panoramic views as well as for the striking cliffs, more than 30 metres high, which juts into the sea. Situated between Utah Beach and Omaha Beach, Pointe du Hoc overlooks the two sites and all of the sea area in which the American landing troops had to land. It was considered to be a strategic position by both sides. The Germans had capped the point with two blockhouses and bunkers that served as barracks for the 150 men based at the battery. The guns of which, thanks to the proximity of the radar station at Percée point, could be directed over a range of 20 kilometres. Or at least that was the theory as, by spring 1944, all the pieces of artillery with which the battery should have been equipped, had yet to be installed, while other components had been removed. Nevertheless, for the Allies, ignorant of its weaknesses, Pointe du Hoc was a place to be taken at all costs. During the night of June 5-6, a deluge of bombs and shells fell on Pointe du Hoc. Over 700 tonnes of bombs were dropped by 125 aeroplanes, while the battleship *Texas* pounded it with more than 600 shots. By 7.10am, Colonel Rudder launched 225 of his rangers to attack the rocky headland. They had spent weeks training on the cliffs of the Isle of Wight, which had many similarities with the French geography.

Top left: **D-Day:** bombing of Pointe du Hoc by A-20's from US 9th Air Force. (U.S.I.S. document) (Taken from *6 juin 1944, débarquement en Normandie*, Général Compagnon, Éd. Ouest-France)

Bottom left: **Pointe du Hoc** juts into the sea like the prow of a ship.

Below: **Pointe de la Percée,** to the east of Pointe du Hoc, carried a radar station that guided the German gunfire.

Pointe du Hoc.
On the site of the artillery command post, a commemorative monument with a simple granite needle has been erected.

Divided into three companies, the assailants didn't even have time to attach ropes or ladders before being hit by a barrage of German bullets and grenades. So severe was the battering that the site had undergone during the night that the whole terrain had been altered. The characteristics of the place, noted and learnt by heart, had been modified by shell holes, beams and tangled pieces of concrete… Indeed the top of the point, now razed, had been reduced in height. But the battery resisted. 135 of the 225 rangers were taken out of combat. The intervention of the commandos of the American 116th infantry regiment was eventually needed to bring an end to the terrible fighting, attacks and counterattacks. The position finally fell on June 8 when new reinforcements arrived. Of the original Ranger force, there were no more than 90 men fit enough for combat by that time. And, at the end of it, it was discovered Pointe du Hoc was an unnecessary diversion. The cannons, dismantled a few days before the landings, had been replaced by large wooden beams.

The artificial harbours

Omaha Beach, in the days that followed D-Day, would become an artificial port.

To send 300,000 men into enemy territory necessitates the simultaneous establishment of an infrastructure big enough to ensure continuous support. The Allies' choice to avoid attacking and recapturing the major ports first required them to construct an artificial harbour for receiving men and heavy equipment in safely and, just as importantly, in quantity.

Nicknamed "mulberries", the artificial harbours were named after berries, as the hundreds of cases of prefabricated concrete that made up the dykes, resembled the intertwining of berry bushes. Each case (60 metres long, 18 metres high, 15 metres wide and weighing 6,000 tonnes), was codenamed "Phoenix" and had been towed from Britain towards the Normandy coast and assembled in the lee of breakwaters created by scuttled boats, codenamed "gooseberries".

Opposite the beach of Saint-Laurent-sur-Mer, on June 8 the Americans began the construction of Mulberry A. But on June 19, a storm destroyed most of the work. Force 7 winds pushed the breakers through the gaps that gave access to the beaches and the anchors were swept away. Floating free, the gooseberries soon broke up. Three days later, nearly 800 boats were washed up on the beach. The whole operation had to be started again.

The wounded are evacuated from Arromanches. (Taken from *Les plages du débarquement*, Yves Lecouturier, Éd. Ouest-France)

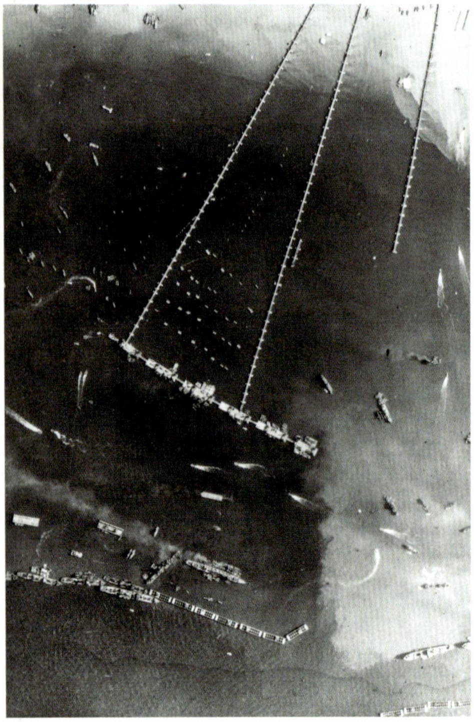

Aerial view of the artificial ports. (Taken from *Les plages du débarquement*, Yves Lecouturier, Éd. Ouest-France)

Concrete Phoenix caissons were sunk to form sheltering jetties.

Arromanches, site of the British artificial port.

Twelve extra blockships were sunk and 26 new Phoenixes were brought in so that work could recommence. But this time the Americans also built floating causeways as well as floating pontoons (codenamed Whales).

Once the weather calmed, and despite the considerable damage, the artificial port of Omaha continued to function, and indeed steadily improved: in February 1945, it was estimated that nearly 600,000 men and more than 100,000 vehicles and engines had passed through it.

The Phoenixes, towed from England, measuring 68 metres long, 18 metres high and weighing nearly 6,000 tonnes.

Asnelles-sur-Mer marked the limit of the artificial harbour of Arromanches.

Gold Beach

IIt was barely 7.25am when General Graham's 50th infantry division, 25,000 impressively trained men who had served in Sicily, landed on the 5 kilometre-long beach that separated Ver-sur-Mer from Asnelles. They were followed by the 8th armoured tank division and its famous "funnies" – designed to overcome the problem of mines, flame-throwing tanks and tank-dozers. Their objective was to take Arromanches, followed by Bayeux. Unfortunately, the currents had diverted them off course by 5 kilometres.

The Mont-Fleury battery, on the cliff overlooking the site, and the Mare Fontaine battery, had been silenced that morning, wiped out by cross-fire from the air force and the navy. From the Ver-sur-Mer side, the operations continued relatively easily and, from mid-morning onwards, the British flag was flying more than a kilometre from the coast. It was a different story at Asnelles, where the Germans, cornered in the Hamel forts, mounted a fierce resistance. The 231st brigade were forced a little to the East in order to find a way through, taking advantage of the lack of motivation among the Russians conscripted into the German army, who wasted no time in fleeing.

Aerial photo taken from an RAF Mustang over Gold Beach at 9am on D-Day. (RAF Museum, Hendon document) (Taken from *6 juin 1944, débarquement en Normandie*, Général Compagnon, Éd. Ouest-France)

By the end of the morning, the Tommies had cleared the beaches and were marching towards Arromanches. They still had to take Saint-Côme-le-Fresné, but its radar station and batteries had been destroyed several days before the landings, and so liberation was achieved that afternoon.

Finally, the British tanks turned towards Arromanches itself, which fell at the start of the evening.

On the beach at Asnelles-sur-Mer, a famous monument in memory of the 231st British infantry brigade.

The first goal had been achieved. They could now move on to the next two, capturing Bayeux and building the artificial harbour that would enable them to supply the Allied troops while waiting for the liberation of a large port.

The same design as the one at Omaha Beach, Mulberry B was the second artificial harbour of the landings. Constructed opposite Arromanches-les-Bains, it was nicknamed Port Winston, in homage to Churchill who, it was said, had the idea for these harbours. A vast bay of some 500 hectares began to take shape on June 7. Work continued on the harbour for a further 12 days, until before it was severely battered by the storms that were simultaneously causing serious damage to Mulberry A, at Saint-Laurent-sur-Mer. At the end of the battle of Normandy, 2,500,000 men, 500,000 vehicles and engines and 4 million tonnes of equipment had passed through the harbour which, for several weeks, had the role of being France's number one port.

Situated at the edge of the British and American zones, Port-en-Bessin was dauntingly protected by an impressive collection of German defences. Fierce resistance meant the town was not liberated until June 8. By the end of June it had become the main land terminal for the "Pipe Line Under the Ocean", codenamed "Pluto", a supply pipeline which received up to 7,500 tonnes of petrol per day from the pumping stations situated on the Isle of Wight.

Port-en-Bessin, a small traditional port, would become the land-based terminal of an underwater pipeline.

Bernières-sur-Mer liberated by the Canadians, including many from Quebec.
Bottom: **Landings at Bernières, June 6 1944.** (Taken from *Les plages du débarquement*, Yves Lecouturier, Éd. Ouest-France)

Juno Beach

The zone from Graye-sur-Mer to Luc-sur-Mer had been left to the Canadians, supported by the British. The Canadians had had a strong desire for revenge ever since Dieppe, when 4,300 of their men were either killed, injured or went missing. Their mission: to take Caen.

The bad weather held up the landing operations and it wasn't until nearly 8am that the men under General Keller, in charge of the Canadian 3rd infantry division, could set foot on the beach of Saint-Aubin-sur-Mer. Some 15,000 Canadians and 9,000 British troops were met with fierce resistance. As well as the 14,000 mines that had been planted there, every possible and imaginable obstacle held up their progress. In particular, the German garrison stranded in their barracks in the "Nan" red sector, who would only give up the fight at the end of the afternoon, after some bloody fighting.

The beach of Bernières-sur-Mer, had been transformed by the Germans into a booby-trapped

It was at Courseulles-sur-Mer that, on June 14, General de Gaulle returned to French soil. Two days earlier, at the same place, Churchill had come ashore, and two days later, King George VI would also land there.

nightmare, and it too would become a landing-craft cemetery: nearly a hundred vehicles would come to grief under a barrage of shellfire. Despite this, the commune was taken by mid-morning.

Langrune-sur-Mer, a few kilometres away, would be more difficult to capture. And despite the courage of Lieutenant-Colonel Moulton's men, the relentless fire from the German batteries meant the little town was not liberated until the following day.

With any resistance from Langrune and Saint-Aubin diminished, the route to Caen would be open. However, it was still necessary to pass through Douvres-la-Délivrande, with its radars capable of surveying the sea to a range of 300 kilometres. The bombardments of the first days of June, and the intensive fire of the morning of June 6, were not enough to nullify its harmful potential. Only the excellence of the British forces render deaf and dumb the Würzburg, the marvel of German surveillance technology, which consequently would not see the invincible armada appear on the Normandy coast. However, it would take 10 more days of combat and eventually gas being pumped into the ventilation system before the complete surrender of the 200 men who were holding the position.

The arrival of the tanks at Courseulles-sur-Mer was difficult: of the 40 that landed, 34 were lost. Every house in every street of the little port had to be taken one by one. At 10.30am, the town was liberated. The position was an important one: the mouth of Seulles would become the main port for supplying the Allies. Twelve boats (gooseberries) were sunk to form a dyke behind which 2,000 tonnes of provisions would eventually arrive.

It was between Courseulles-sur-Mer and Graye-sur-Mer that, on June 14, General de Gaulle disembarked from *La Combattante*, setting foot on French soil after four years of exile. Two days earlier, at the same place, Churchill had come ashore, and two days later, King George VI who also land there.

A German battery could strafe the Saint-Aubin-sur-Mer beach from on high, at the place known as La Cassine.

Landings at Hermanville-sur-Mer, June 6 1944. (Taken from *Les plages du débarquement*, Yves Lecouturier, Éd. Ouest-France)

Sword Beach

The British 3rd infantry division, commanded by Major General T. Rennie, set foot on the section of beach between Colleville-sur-Orne and Ouistreham at 7.30am. Its objective was to liaise with the 6th airborne division at Pegasus Bridge, who had liberated the right bank of the Orne and, with the Canadians, advance on to Caen, which must be captured by the end of the day.

Luc-sur-Mer was the oldest seaside resort on the Calvados coast. The beach, a mixture of sand

Orne Estuary.

Hermanville, liberated on June 6 at 10 am.

and pebbles, was backed by a cliff, on the flanks and the summit of which the Germans had built numerous defences. It would not be until June 7, after a bloody battle at the place named "Little Hell", that Luc-sur-Mer would be liberated.

The landing at Hermanville was a happier one. The wind was strong but the barges arrived on time, at the intended place, and the losses were limited: 21 of the 25 amphibious tanks reached the beach. While the men of the South Lancashire regiment liberated the town mid-morning, Admiral Wietzel scuttles the *Gustave Courbet* which, along with other warships and cargo ships, would form the breakwaters enabling the disembarkation of men and equipment in safe conditions.

Hermanville had suffered relatively little from the advance bombings.

At Biéville, on the road to Caen, the 12th *Panzerdivision* held up the Allies for over a month.

Right and below: **Ouistreham and Riva Bella.** It was here that the Kieffer commando made their name, the only French soldiers to take part in the Landings.

Colleville-sur-Orne harboured a formidable German defensive complex, the Hillman site: 12 concrete units, linked together by 600 metres of underground passages, protected with barbed wire, equipped with machine guns and surrounded by thousands of mines. It took the whole day and two bloody attempts before General Rennie's men achieved their goal.

After the war, Colleville-sur-Orne changed its name to Colleville-Montgomery, in recognition of General Montgomery, who beat Rommel at El Alamein and was Eisenhower's deputy for the Normandy landings.

At the start of the morning, the Franco-British 4th commando, under the command of Lieutenant Commander Philippe Kieffer, lands at the edge of the long beach of Riva Bella, on the West bank of the Orne. These 117 naval fusiliers represent the only French unit to set foot on national soil on June 6. The first objective assigned to them was to neutralize the German defences on the Riva Bella.

In 1942, the Germans had destroyed the Ouistreham casino to build in its place the "Big Bunker", which, at 17 metres high, overlooked the mouth of the Orne and controlled the various Ouistreham batteries. With the support of the armoured tanks, Kieffer's men took the bunker by mid-morning but at great cost. By 1pm, only 60 men were still standing.

At nightfall, while the air force bombarded Douvres-la-Délivrande, Luc-sur-Mer and Lion-sur-Mer, where German resistance was continuing, *Operation Mallard* was launched: 250 British gliders release reinforcements of men and hundreds of thousands of tonnes of equipment over various parts of the Orne. The Germans act quickly. General Feuchtinger, commander of the 21st *Panzerdivision,* mounts a counterattack. But it was in vain. However, by that night, the British and Canadian victories, admirable though they were, do not include the neutralisation of the Carpiquet aerodrome and, crucially, the capturing of Caen.

Sainte-Mère-Eglise, the first French village to be liberated, on June 6, at 4.30am. John Steel spent the whole night hanging by his parachute from the tower of the church.

The first liberated towns

Sainte-Mère-Eglise

Around 12.30am, on June 6 1944, under the deafening sound of hundreds of low-flying planes, the sky over Sainte-Mère-Eglise was filled with what looked like thousands of white daisies falling to earth. If the sky had been clear and the weather a little better, it could have been said that there were thousands of shooting stars. The reality was 13,000 men from the American 101st airborne division had just jumped from their planes, their mission to secure the exits of Utah Beach. Most of them were inexperienced. It was their first "real" engagement after months of training. The violent winds that night dispersed them over an area at least 45 kilometres long and 25 wide. Those who landed to the East fell between woodland and marsh. They were not prepared for this kind of environment, and it proved to be full of natural traps such as hedges in which they became entangled, laden down with heavy equipment. The general in charge – General Maxwell Taylor – was himself lost. Out of the 13,000, there were barely 6,000 men fit for combat on the ground.

General Matthew D. Ridgway's 82nd airborne division had more success, even though they were dropped into a heavily defended area. These men, more experienced in war than their comrades in the 101st, having served in Sicily, all land within a 5-kilometre square. One of them, soldier John Steel, would become an involuntary hero with the painful and sublime image of the parachutist hanging from the spire of the church while the bells sounded the alarm and, at his feet, the battle rages.

At 4am, some 50 gliders landed to the North of Hiesville, laden with reinforcements but also with a surgical unit, while some 50 others landed on a stone jetty, to the Northwest of Sainte-Mère-Eglise.

At 4.30am, the 3rd battalion of the 505th regiment of the 82nd airborne division liberated Sainte-Mère-Eglise after violent battles against the 91st division of the Luftwaffe. The American flag flies over the town hall just two hours before the landings. However, bitter battles, sometimes, man-to-man, would continue until 7am and the arrival of the first tanks on Utah Beach.

Bayeux

Miraculously undamaged by the Allied bombardment, Bayeux was

the first major French town to be liberated: on the morning of June 7, the British 30th corps, haven taken Arromanches the previous evening, entered the town to little resistance.

Some 15 kilometres from the coast, Bayeux has always had a turbulent history, with Bretons, Saxons and Normans all living within its walls, long before the Germans arrived. It was also the point of departure for the conquest of England in 1066, by William, duke of Normandy, the story of which is told in the famous 70-metre long tapestry, also known as the "Queen Mathilde tapestry".

In June 1944, it was another conquest, or rather reconquest, that began in Bayeux. Landing on June 14 between Courseulles-sur-Mer and Graye-sur-Mer, General de Gaulle was welcomed to Bayeux in jubilation by 2,000 people. He had just forced the hand of the Allies – and Roosevelt particularly – who believed liberated France would be under the authority of AMGOT (*Allied Military Government of Occupied Territories*) as was the case in Italy. The same day, the fourth anniversary of the German entry into Paris, General de Gaulle set up the government of liberated France and declared: "I hereby declare without further ado that the enemy has fled and the authority of my government has been restored. The republican power is, as of now, re-established."

Top: **The former Bayeux seminary** where the famous tapestry is exhibited.

Bottom: **Bayeux,** liberated the morning of June 7, miraculously unharmed.

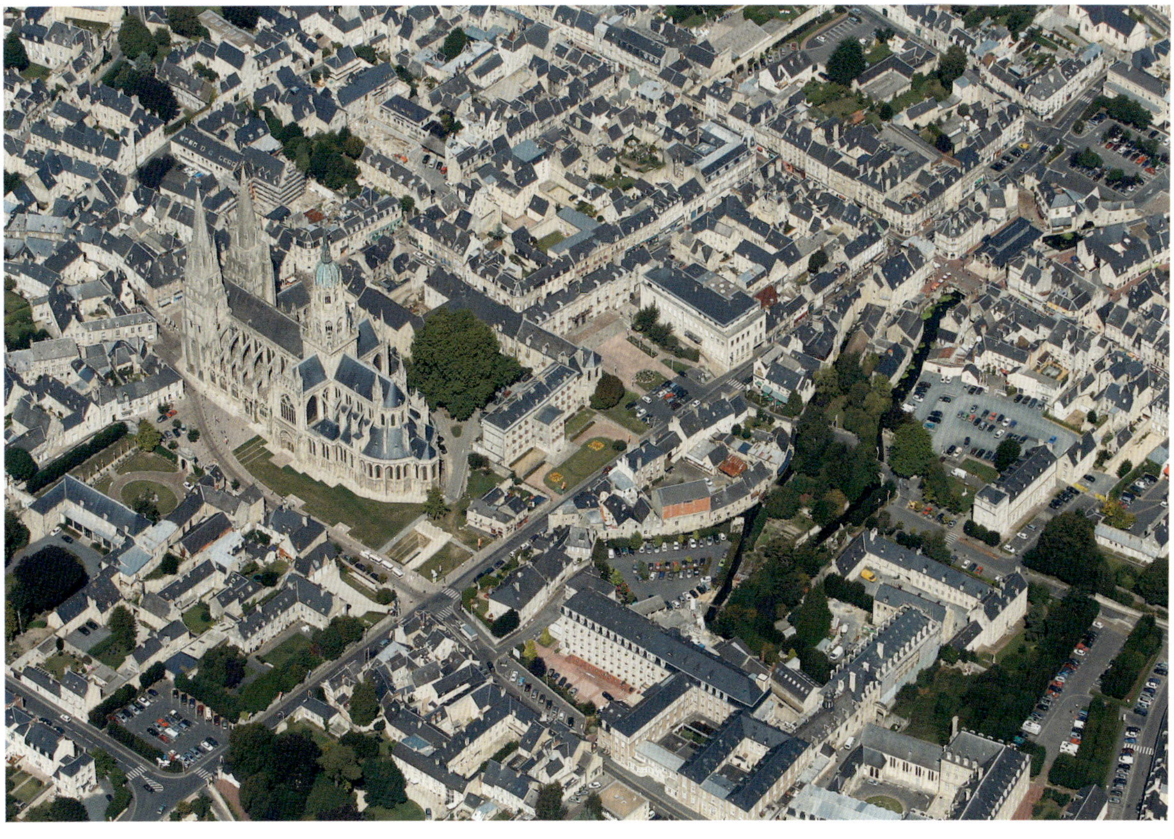

Caen

The Allies planned to capture Caen on the evening of June 6. The town had been heavily bombed during the night of June 5-6. But, despite their courage and some notable successes, British and Canadian troops were intercepted that evening by the 21st *Panzerdivision*, six kilometres from the Normandy capital. The Germans mounted a ferocious defence, aware of the strategic importance of Caen. They took no prisoners: from 10.30am onwards on June 6, they shot between 70 and 75 Resistance members who were being held in the town prison.

Caen, July 1944: the Saint-Pierre church after the victory, damaged on June 9 by a "40" from cruiser *HMS Rodney*. (E.C.P.A. document) (Taken from *6 juin 1944, débarquement en Normandie*, Général Compagnon, Éd. Ouest-France)

The exact number of summary executions is difficult to estimate, as the bodies were never found. The 12th SS *Hitlerjugend* division, based in Evreux, was swiftly deployed to the Northwest of the town. The bombings recommenced on June 7 and it seemed as though they would never end. The town was ravaged by fires and shelling for ten days. Thousands of Caen's residents took refuge in the Abbaye-aux-Hommes, a Roman-Gothic architectural masterpiece. Thus, the monastic building was reprieved from the destruction, and also went on to serve as a medical centre. This was not to be the case for its sister abbey, the Abbaye-aux-Femmes, nor William the Conqueror's chateau, both of which were badly hit. On June 10 Hitler orders that: "Every man must fight and fall on the spot." If the enemy could not be immediately dispatched back to the beachheads, it was at least vital to gain some time. Hitler was waiting impatiently for his infamous new weapons that he hoped would make the Allies give back their ill-gotten gains: in the night of June 12-13 the first V-1 bombs were launched over London.

The British and Canadians increased their attacks but it was in vain. The bombardments continued. On July 7, 450 bombers dropped 2,500 tonnes of bombs. Two-thirds of the town were laid to ruin. On July 8 the Canadians were able to enter the devastated Northern quarters. It would take a further 10 days of *Operation Goodwood,* centred on the course of the little Odon river, a new deluge of shelling, violent gunfire and man-to-man combat, before the SS of the 12th *Hitlerjugend* and the 272nd infantry division would be defeated. On July 19, Caen was liberated.

Centre: **Caen, the Abbaye-aux-Hommes,** restored after the two hellish months of the 1944 siege.
Bottom: **The Caen chateau,** a fortress established by William the Conqueror.

Saint-Lô

The main base of the German 84th army corps, Saint-Lô occupied a strategic position to the South of the Cotentin peninsula from where it controlled one of the main access points to the region. As an important crossroads, the town became a communications nerve centre of which it would be vital to gain control.

Like Caen, Saint-Lô should have been captured on June 6. In order to do this, more than 5,000 tonnes of bombs transformed the town into a "capital of ruins". But the Germans held strong, all the more so because the Americans, the worse for wear after Utah and Omaha, struggled to make their way across the land. Their worst enemy were the thick hedges, not something with which they were familiar. The Germans, after four years, had got used to them and used them wisely. These embankments, undisturbed by the shelling and capped with a dense and bushy vegetation, formed an impenetrable maze that the tanks could not cross. The infantrymen had to clear the route, lane-by-lane, hedge-by-hedge, embankment-by-embankment. In 12 days, the American 8th army progressed only 11 kilometres. At this point, a sergeant had the idea of attaching a plough to the front of the tanks, thereby transforming them into bulldozers that would flatten the embankments and other obstacles.

End of July 1944: Saint-Lô in ruins after the vicious battles that resulted in its liberation by the Americans on July 19. (R.H.A. document) (Taken from *6 juin 1944, débarquement en Normandie*, Général Compagnon, Éd. Ouest-France)

While the battle was raging in Caen, the Americans captured the poorly defended Cherbourg on June 27. But Saint-Lô was still resisting. On July 12, the Americans were positioned high above the town. Four army corps were charged with holding this zone. On July 17, General Middleton's men seized Pont-Hébert, 6 kilometres away. On the 18, the 115th regiment entered the ruins of the ghost town and, by July 19, Saint-Lô, or what was left of it, was "liberated". Nothing remained of the town apart from a few houses in the suburbs and the remnants of the Notre-Dame collegiate.

Saint-Lô, left in ruins in 1944, has been entirely rebuilt.

In Memory

Liberty has a price and the recapture of this territory cost dear. From June 6 to the end of July 1944, it was estimated that more than 600,000 men were either killed, missing, injured or prisoners of war. It was the Germans that suffered the heaviest losses: nearly two thirds of the total figure. The cemeteries bear silent witness to this along the length of the Normandy coast and around some of the towns further inland.

British Military Cemetery, Bayeux

The greatest number of Tommies lie in Bayeux: 4,382 British graves as well as 466 others, some Germans and some of other nationalities. Opposite the cemetery, on a majestic portico, are the names of the 1,807 missing, engraved in the white marble. At the base, a Latin phrase recounts how the British nation came in 1944 to liberate the country that had defeated it in 1066.

Canadian Cemetery, Bény-Reviers

Straddling two communes, Bény-sur-Mer and Reviers, there are 2,044 gravestones, simply decorated with a maple leaf, recalling the memory of the fallen Canadians. 335 of them belonged to the Major-General Keller's 3rd division, which landed on June 6 at Juno. A further 1,709, including 15 pilots, from diverse units, fell during interior battles in the liberation of Normandy.

American Military Cemetery, Colleville-sur-Mer

On the cliff overlooking Omaha Beach, the American cemetery of Colleville-sur-Mer is by far the largest of all the Allied cemeteries. 9,386 Italian marble gravestones, in the form of crosses or stars of David, are lined up in eerie silence. On the Wall of the Missing, a white circle bears the names of 1,557 men. At the centre of the memorial, Donald de Lue's monumental sculpture represents the eternity of American youth.

Polish Cemetery, Langannerie

On the route between Caen and Falaise, where the Allies' advance came to an abrupt halt between August 8-10 1944, on the exact spot where the battles took place, is the location of the only Polish cemetery of the landings, at Langannerie, near Urville. 650 graves of soldiers from the General Maczek's Polish 1st armoured tank division can be found there. Equipped with Sherman tanks, it was their first engagement in the battle of Normandy.

Deutsche Soldaten Friedhof, La Cambe

It was Germany that suffered most heavily during the difficult and glorious hours of the landings. 115,000 bodies were found wearing the Wehrmacht uniform. Of these, some now lie in the Allies' cemeteries but most were placed together in burial places dedicated to German soldiers. There are five main ones. The La Cambe cemetery is the biggest of these, with 21,202 bodies, 21,202 little gravestones placed on the short grass, in the shade of large trees, simply laid out in groups of five plain stone crosses. At the centre of the necropolis is a mound topped with a large cross and two large figures, serving as a memorial to the 296 unknown soldiers.

A selection of museums, memorials and other Landings sites

Calvados

Musée du Débarquement
Place du 6-Juin
14117 ARROMANCHES
Tel. + 33 (0) 2 31 22 34 31
www.normandie1944.fr

Mémorial du Général de Gaulle
10 rue Bourbesneur
14400 BAYEUX
Tel. + 33 (0) 2 31 92 45 55

Musée Mémorial de la Bataille de Normandie
Boulevard Fabian-Ware
14400 BAYEUX
Tel. + 33 (0) 2 31 51 46 90

Mémorial de Caen
Esplanade Eisenhower
14000 CAEN
Tel. + 33 (0) 2 31 06 06 45
www.memorial-caen.fr

Centre Juno Beach
Voie des Français-Libres
BP 104 14470 COURSEULLES-SUR-MER
Tel. + 33 (0) 2 31 37 32 17
www.junobeach.org

Musée du Radar
Route Basly
14440 DOUVRES-LA-DÉLIVRANDE
Tel. + 33 (0) 231 37 74 43

Musée Août 44
Chemin des Roches
14700 FALAISE
Tel. + 33 (0) 2 31 90 37 19
www.normandie-museeaout44.com

Musée des Rangers
Quai Crampon
14450 GRANDCAMP-MAISY
Tel. + 33 (0) 2 31 92 33 51

Batterie de Longues-sur-Mer
14400 LONGUES-SUR-MER
Tel. + 33 (0) 2 31 21 46 87

Musée de la Batterie de Merville
Place du 9e-Bataillon
14810 MERVILLE-FRANCEVILLE
Tel. + 33 (0) 2 31 91 47 53
www.batterie-merville.com

Musée du Mur de l'Atlantique
Avenue du 6-Juin
14150 OUISTREHAM
Tel. + 33 (0) 2 31 97 28 69
www.le-grand-bunker-musee.com

Musée N° 4 Commando
Place Alfred-Thomas
14150 OUISTREHAM
Tel. + 33 (0) 2 31 96 63 10

Musée des Epaves sous-marines du Débarquement
Route de Bayeux – Commes
14520 PORT-EN-BESSIN-HUPPAIN
Tel. + 33 (0) 2 31 21 17 06

Mémorial Pégasus
Avenue du Major-Howard
14860 RANVILLE
Tel. + 33 (0) 2 31 78 19 44
www.normandie1944.fr

Musée Mémorial Omaha Beach
« Les Moulins »
Avenue de la Libération
14710 SAINT-LAURENT-SUR-MER
Tel. + 33 (0) 2 31 21 97 44
www.musee-memorial-omaha.com

Musée de la Percée du Bocage
D. 675
14350 SAINT-MARTIN-DES-BESACES
Tel. + 33 (0) 2 31 67 52 78
www.laperceedubocage.com

Musée America Gold Beach
2 place Amiral-Byrd
14114 VER-SUR-MER
Tel. + 33 (0) 2 31 22 58 58

Musée D-Day Omaha
Route de Grandcamp-Maisy
14710 VIERVILLE-SUR-MER
Tel. + 33 (0) 231 21 71 80
www.dday-omaha.net